THE
Castle
Church

Written by Kristen Comello
Illustrated by Jeri Lochmann

www.nofloss.com

Independent Publisher; December 2014

Manufactured in the United States of America

** Special thanks to Anthea Ancalade of ASBA Creative Studio (www.asbacreativestudio.com) for the book design. **

ISBN 978-0-98632870-1

Dedication to My Grandma
Jeri Lochmann, Illustrator

My Grandma is full blooded Italian-American with a heart of gold. She has lived her life devoted to God and his teachings. She raised eight kids and has many grandkids, great grandkids, and great-great grand kids.

God has blessed her over the years, and she has responded by teaching young, old, and even prisoners how great God's love is for all people. As a devoted Catholic, she taught Junior High CCD (a religious program for children) for five years, RCIA for seven years, and Life Teen for ten years. She ran the Confirmation program for twenty years, the music program for all masses for 21 years, sang in the church choir since age 10. She went to Catholic Congress every year for 17 years to get certified. The list goes on. She has helped many people young and old open the doors to a new path of life with God. She currently is active in prison ministry. She started when she was in her seventies and still does it at 84. During her passion for teaching others about God, she always made time for her family and grand kids.

My Grandma has so many talents and now I can add Artist to the list. She has catered, sewn all her kids' clothes, designed wardrobes for Priests, was an opera singer and the most crafty lady I know. She still amazes me as her talents never stop overflowing.

She and my Grandpa have the most impressive love through God. They taught us how to love your spouse till the end of time with grace. They love each other now more than ever. They gave me a strong sense of family. They are the example of unconditional love. I have learned that you never give up on the people you love. It may take forty years of prayer, but God can do anything and in his time prayers are answered.

Thank you Grandma for your love, creativity, good food, your example of living faith, and your complete devotion to God. I am so lucky to have such a strong, beautiful woman to look up to, whose love is always there and unconditional. I love you till the ends of the earth and up in heaven with God.

THE
Castle
Church

Hi! I'm Britesen (*Bright-sen*), it's Sunday, and my mom, dad, brothers (Alek and Luke) and I are going to Church. My Church is the Catholic Church in Monterey, California. It is called San Carlos Cathedral, The Royal Presidio Chapel, but I call it the Castle Church. I like going to the Castle Church.

We always go through the secret door. On the way, there is a fountain. We always drop a penny in it, but instead of making a wish, we say a prayer. It's like a wish because we want it to come true.

When we walk to Church, we dip our hands in Holy Water and make the sign of the cross saying, "In the name of the Father, Son, and Holy Spirit, Amen."

When mass starts, an altar server walks in with a big cross and leads the Priest to the altar. The Priest blesses us and says a prayer.

I like to be early for Church so I can walk up to the altar with all the other kids. On the way out we sing, "We are the Church, happy to be." It is a fun song with clapping and then we go to Children's Church.

When my mommy is late we go straight to Children's Church and I miss singing with my friends.

I am so excited because I like Children's Church. I learn about God and his life in the Bible with my friends. We sing songs and have fun.

In Children's Church, we say hello and
then close our eyes and say a prayer. I have a hard
time keeping my eyes closed so I leave them open.

It's Bible story time. Today's story is about a man named Lazarus. Lazarus was a good friend of Jesus. He was very sick and died. Don't worry -- this story has a happy ending! Jesus goes to the tomb where Lazarus was buried. He tells Lazarus to get up and walk. Lazarus was alive.

In Children's Church, I was chosen to be wrapped up like Lazarus with toilet paper. We decided that he must have hopped out of the tomb because his legs were wrapped up like a mummy.

When I get older and I have a dog of my own, I want
to name him Lazarus after Jesus' best friend.
I will love my dog like Jesus loved Lazarus.

Now it's time to go back to the big Church.
My brothers are too little to follow me, so they go
back to Church through the secret door with my mom.

Sometimes I get to carry presents and the collection up to Jesus' table. Then it is the time for the bread and wine to be changed into Jesus. He fills us with love and makes us strong and happy.

My favorite time of the Mass is when we say the "Our Father." I know this prayer because my brothers and I say it every night before we go to bed.

After saying the "Our Father", we shake hands in the "Sign of Peace". My Nanu (*grandfather*) taught me how to shake hands before I could walk. I am good at this. I shake everyone's hand in my row.

When it's communion time, I am too small to receive God's blessed bread. Instead, I go up to the altar with my arms crossed over my heart and get a blessing.

When mass is over, we go to the hall.

It is Holy Doughnut time.
Oh yeah! Oh yeah! Oh yeah!
I love Holy Doughnuts every Sunday.

We go to Church to show our love to God, Jesus, and the Holy Spirit. Sometimes my skin tingles and it makes my heart happy.

After church, if we have been good, we get to go to the Dennis The Menace Park. I love Church, donuts, and the park. Sunday is always a fun day with God.

Made in the USA
Columbia, SC
23 February 2024

32148988R00024